T0137502

The *Heart Unseen*

Revealed, Revived, Restored
(1 Samuel 25:2-42)

TONI S. TROXELL

WESTBOW
PRESS®
A DIVISION OF THOMAS NELSON
& ZONDERVAN

WestBow Press books may be ordered through booksellers or by contacting:

WestBow Press
A Division of Thomas Nelson & Zondervan
1663 Liberty Drive
Bloomington, IN 47403
www.westbowpress.com
1 (866) 928-1240

Because of the dynamic nature of the Internet, any web addresses or links contained in this book may have changed since publication and may no longer be valid. The views expressed in this work are solely those of the author and do not necessarily reflect the views of the publisher, and the publisher hereby disclaims any responsibility for them.

Any people depicted in stock imagery provided by Getty Images are models, and such images are being used for illustrative purposes only.
Certain stock imagery © Getty Images.

All Scripture quotations are taken from the New King James Version®. Copyright © 1982 by Thomas Nelson. Used by permission. All rights reserved.

ISBN: 978-1-9736-7897-7 (sc)
ISBN: 978-1-9736-7898-4 (hc)
ISBN: 978-1-9736-7896-0 (e)

Library of Congress Control Number: 2019917827

Print information available on the last page.

WestBow Press rev. date: 11/5/2019

To my son, Charlie

God gave you to me, and I am humbled every day at the wonderful servant of God you are. God allows us to have special people in our lives, and He gave you into mine. Serve Him well, my son, as you have continued to do. And to God be all the glory!

Contents

Acknowledgments

What a privilege God gives us to study His Word and, on top of that, to apply His written Word to our lives. All the glory and praise go to my heavenly Father who gave His only Son for our sins, the Lord Jesus Christ, and allows His Holy Spirit to guide every area of my life. Without You, Father, I can do nothing, so to You, Almighty God, I give the glory for every word, every thought, and any blessings someone may receive from this book.

Preface

It's amazing what humans can do. I mean, think about Legos. Isn't it amazing what a person can build out of those things? One piece looks like another until you begin to put them all together. Then wow! An amazing structure emerges. Moving parts … and the detail! What a masterpiece! What you build simply depends on your imagination and the right choices of pieces.

People are amazing. We may begin on pretty much common ground, yet as each page unfolds and our lives grow, the masterpiece we will become depends on the choices we will make. As a child of God in the Master's hand, Jesus Christ our Savior molds our hearts, minds, and souls. When we allow our Lord to take the pieces and put them together, there are no limits.

As people, our hearts and our inner souls are complex. We may think we keep our hearts from being seen, but the

God of all the universe sees everything, even the invisible parts no one else does. Our hearts may be invisible to the world, but not to almighty God. When we no longer see God as God, we need reminders of His greatness. What the enemy, Satan, wants is for us to make choices that forget God and chase after our own way.

If he can keep us distracted, we become powerless, unfruitful, and lifeless. Many Christians live as though our God lives in a box or a bottle. Our distorted view comes from a sinful and stained world. We put God on our level, in our closet, and expect Him to dance when we sing. This book will take us on a journey to see, learn, and apply what can happen when we are yielded and when we are not to almighty God. When we allow our hearts to be filled and yielded to our God, oh, the possibilities!

1 Samuel 25:2–42[1] is an amazing story of how God moves mountains, deals with the scoundrels in our lives, restores, protects, and gives us the wisdom we need to face all sorts of obstacles. Join me as we learn together that though we may be limited, we may have boundaries, we may have struggles, and it may be hard, "but God" can do it all. *The Heart Unseen* reveals what God can do with a willing heart. Brace yourself. You may climb that wall yet.

---

[1] The Holy Bible: New King James Version (Nashville: Thomas Nelson, 1982).

Chapter 1

Building a Résumé (Who Are You?)

A résumé is a collection of events and explanations of experiences in a person's life. When a person applies for a job, he or she will often produce a résumé to show experience. The surprising thing is that everyone has a résumé. And each person has three things in common on these résumés: a beginning, a middle, and an end. Some are longer than average; others are shorter. The question is this: when God reads your résumé of life, what will it say? And He will read it (Romans 14:11–13).

From the moment God puts each person on this planet, his or her résumé begins to take form, and He has a plan for each of us (Jeremiah 29:11). The résumé of our lives begins to take shape the moment God has us in the womb. As we grow, those who have charge over us, such as guardians or parents, begin to write on our résumés. However, somewhere along the line we take over the writing. No matter what has been written before, once we take over the writing, it is all on us. Yes, of course there are those experiences we would rather not have—disappointments, heartaches, betrayals, and so forth—yet these make us the unique people we are. We must resolve that we will use those experiences to create a better picture, a brighter image. Each experience builds on the last to design and draw a beautiful picture of where we were and where we are headed.

When I look back over my life, I am totally amazed from where God has brought me. As God writes out each page, we make choices. We can allow these experiences—no matter what they are—to lead us away from the path God has for us or lead us on the road He has paved. Who we are and who we will become depend on what we decide along the way. Let me ask you a question: what in your heart keeps your résumé from painting the beautiful you? Is it hurt, bitterness, loneliness, anger, betrayal, or a bit of each?

Although no human sees your precious heart, God does. That is important for you and me to know. Why? In the shadow of our hearts, in the deep, dark tunnels, we hide those things that keep us from being all that God would have us be. Opening those tunnels is what God our Father wants to do.

First Samuel 25: 2–42 reveals the heart of three individuals. For these three people, their résumés have been written. There are of course others in the picture who are important; however, our focus here is on three distinct people: David, a soon-to-be king; Nabal, a harsh and evildoing man; and Abigail, Nabal's wife, who is wise and of good understanding. Each of these individuals has written a résumé in which we can glean a harvest of lessons if we are willing to be honest with ourselves and God.

A series of circumstances brought David, Nabal, and Abigail together, and not one of them could have dreamed the outcome. Only God knew the outcome; only God knew each heart. However, each person would have to make a split-second decision that would change his or her life. We are no different.

I have a little background before we move on. In 1 Samuel 16, David was anointed the new king of Israel after God rejected Saul, the present king. Saul's disobedience to God cost him the throne (1 Samuel 15). And although David did not immediately take the throne, he would eventually become king. Saul, on the other hand, began to resent David (1 Samuel 18–19) and even wanted to take his life because of jealousy. Yet until the right time designed by God, David was on the run. David would eventually acquire a group of men who rode with him (1 Samuel 22), and they spent their days trying to avoid Saul. He was still king after all, and David did not want to fight against God's anointed (1 Samuel 24:6). David had quite the résumé on the run from Saul, with many important decisions to make.

Like David, our early experiences help us learn from successes and failures. This is part of who we are. This is how we determine if we have a heart for God. Every page of that résumé gives a picture of our choices, both good and bad. I don't know about you, but I have made some killer mistakes in my life, especially in my youth. The wonderful part of all these mistakes is that by learning I am not that person any longer, I find that God has given me so many chances to grow and learn from these mistakes. I am eternally grateful to my God. He has allowed me to write new pages to my résumé using these mistakes. What happens on those pages is often up to us.

David came close to making some bad choices, options God that did not have for him and would have been unfortunate. Then there is Nabal. The Bible describes Nabal as a very rich man in Maon who is married to Abigail. He is harsh, of the house of Caleb, and evil in all his doings (1 Samuel 25:2–3). Wow! What a résumé! Quite the man, wouldn't you say? Not someone you want your daughter to marry, right?

As we are about to see, his résumé only gets worse. And the end is tragic. Nabal was unwilling to change the writing of his résumé and to learn from his mistakes. Nabal was Nabal-centered to the end. His hard heart—a heart of stone, you might say—led him right into a brick wall. He was unwilling to move his heart toward God. He had an unwilling, hard heart. How cold and unresponsive a heart like this can be! How lonely!

Then there is Abigail. The Bible describes Abigail as "Nabal's wife, a woman of good understanding and beautiful appearance" (1 Samuel 25:3). Abigail has a lot going for her. Her résumé is impressive. Abigail's résumé is surprising, considering whom she lives with. "Do not be deceived: 'Evil company corrupts good habits'" (1 Corinthians 15:33). They could not be more opposite. He's harsh; she's gentle. He's dishonest; she's truthful. What a pair with two totally different résumés! Yet the Bible shares Abigail in a beautiful light.

And Abigail's résumé only gets better. She is not about to be distracted from the task at hand. Had she been, several innocent people would have died, and a soon-to-be king would have made a terrible decision. A heart for God made the difference.

As I mentioned before, each of these three persons had to make a decision that would alter their lives. We too make these same decisions. Ours may not be as difficult as theirs, but they are life-altering choices nonetheless. When you hand employers your résumé, they are looking for those experiences and training that will help with the job for which you are applying. I would not apply for the job of a doctor since I have no training. As an employer myself, I often find myself searching for the right person to fill a certain position.

I must confess this is one part of my job I do not enjoy. I may go through several résumés before I find the correct person. What lies on the pages of a person's résumé speaks volumes to my search and me. I will often read that cover letter first to determine if that person holds the right qualities for the job. Sometimes I will ask questions like, "What are your plans for the future?" Some are focused and know the plans they have; others have no idea and seem distracted. Applicants can even doctor a résumé and make it look glamorous and appealing, but once I begin to investigate the content, the truth will be revealed.

The résumé we write of our daily lives and the choices we make are revealing more than we may realize. We spend a lifetime writing these résumés. Don't we want them to say the truth of who we are and the choices we have made? I mean once the résumé is complete and it is in the Master's hand, there is no rewriting, no erasing, and no undoing. It is finished. So, shouldn't we begin even now to write a résumé we would want anyone to read? It doesn't matter what is written up to this point. God can make the rest of your pages, and mine becomes a beautiful portrait of lives well lived.

I will say that often when we start to read over our life

résumé, the distractions of regrets and remorse can set us back. Maybe we have not written on the pages as we should. Perhaps we allowed too many distractions to lead us away from the cross. We may not be able to rewrite those pages, but we can write better ones in the future. The reason this is at the front of this book is so we can begin to think about the pages we have written and what we want to record in the future.

Don't Let Dwelling on the Past Trip You Up

Don't dwell on the past. Many people make this mistake. I myself have. "Brethren, I do not count myself to have apprehended; but one thing I do, forgetting those things which are behind and reaching forward to those things which are ahead" (Philippians 3:13).

Getting caught up in the past pages of our lives can distract us from the future God has for us. Don't think for a moment that God can't make the remaining pages of your life spectacular. He most certainly can. This has no age limit. God can do it all. Take your focus off the past and place it in the hand of God who can write a beautiful picture with your remaining pages. Perhaps you do not have a relationship with the God who turns ashes into beauty (Isaiah 61:3). At the end of this book, there is a simple way to have that relationship. Don't let any distraction, not even this book, keep you from turning there now and beginning that relationship. It is called "God's Plan for Salvation."

Your Résumé Is Important

What Will You Be Writing Next?

Remember you are writing your résumé for the God of heaven and earth, for one day we will stand before Him as He reads. Never think for a moment you do not have a résumé or yours has no value. Christ died for you. That makes every page worth the effort.

Let's face it. We all have pages in our résumé we would like to remove; however, each page is who we are. God can take every page and make it beautiful. But that means surrendering the former pages, coming with blank pages, and letting Christ be the Lord of your life. Easy? Absolutely not. A lot of rethinking and the removal of flawed thinking may have to be done.

Removing distractions is never easy but is possible. Almighty God can do it all. Time, prayer, release, and Bible study is all part of the equation of writing those new pages. You can begin right now jotting down your pages to move beyond the place you are. Pray and ask God to help the new pages of your résumé be the best yet.

2 Corinthians 3:3 (NKJV)

"Clearly you are an epistle of Christ, ministered by us, written not with ink but by the Spirit of the living God, not on tablets of stone but on tablets of flesh, that is, of the heart."

Chapter 2

When Opportunity Comes

I n 1 Samuel 25, we have introduced three characters. Each has written a résumé of his or her life, part of which we see in 1 Samuel 25. David is on the run from King Saul. Nabal is rich and tending his home. He is not a nice guy. Abigail, a wise woman, is Nabal's wife. Each is about to make an important decision and has an opportunity to do right or wrong. It is that simple. What we say and do is an opportunity to do right or wrong. Our views and the condition of our heart often determine the decision.

1 Samuel 25:2–3 describe the three people we have mentioned in chapter one. We do not get what each person is totally like; however, we do get an idea of how each person is viewed. As we study the scriptures, it is no secret as to

whom David is or who is he is to become, the future king of Israel. Samuel had anointed him as the Holy Spirits leads, and now he must wait until the time God has set aside for David to rule. Nabal, on the other hand, is a rich man who has a reputation of dealing "evil in his doings" (1 Samuel 25:3). He also is mentioned as a scoundrel in verse 17, which means a cheat, a dishonest man. He is also mentioned as harsh or cruel in verse 3.

Nabal is not spoken well of in the scriptures. How sad! Abigail, his wife, is spoken of in quite a different light. A woman of good understanding, she is wise and beautiful. I am sure her wisdom makes her all the more beautiful. These three individuals are about to have opportunities that will change their lives.

As we open the pages of 1 Samuel 25:2–42, we have already seen the description of our three people. Verse four begins with David, as we mentioned before, on the run from Saul. He is in the wilderness with men who have joined him (1 Samuel 22). Getting food for him and his men is a top priority, and when he hears Nabal is shearing sheep, he knows there would be feasting and celebrating, which would mean plenty of food. And the fact Nabal is mentioned as a rich man means his celebrating would be great.

David sees an opportunity to perhaps get some food for his men and him. So David decides to send ten young men to Nabal to ask for food.

When David heard in the wilderness that Nabal was shearing his sheep, David sent ten young men; and David said to the young men, "Go up to Carmel, go to Nabal, and greet him in my name. And thus you shall say to him who lives in prosperity: 'Peace be to you, peace to your house, and peace to all that you have! Now I have heard that you have shearers. Your shepherds were with us, and we did not hurt them, nor was there anything missing from them all the while they were in Carmel. Ask your young men, and they will tell you. Therefore, let my young men find favor in your eyes, for we come on a feast day. Please give whatever comes to your hand to your servants and to your son David.'" (1 Samuel 25:4–8)

Because it is a time of celebration, David thinks it would be a great time to get food. There would be lots of help for the shearing and food, just an all-around celebration. Surely Nabal would know who David is and willingly offer food for him and his men.

David sends a humble and respectful greeting to Nabal by way of these ten young men. And with the greeting comes a request. David is leader to this group of men who followed him, and he feels responsible for them. And that means shelter and food. David views the circumstance as an opportunity to provide food for his men. David also shares with Nabal that the whole time his shepherds were in the field they never touched them.

Remember these men are hungry, and if you read the description of these men in 1 Samuel 22, you can see that keeping order may at times have been a job for David. Nevertheless, David and his men never harmed them. In fact, David and his men protected Nabal's sheep and shepherds from harm. They became "like a wall" of protection (1 Samuel 25:16).

As instructed by David, the men go to Nabal and share all that David spoke. Then they wait for the answer. Opportunity means that something falls into place and could make something happen. We hear this word all the time in our society. We have opportunities to obtain new jobs, to buy a house, or to help others or not. Opportunities come in all shapes and sizes. Some we seize; others we miss.

In our walk with the Lord, we as Christians are given opportunities daily to help others witness, encourage, give, or neglect. I was standing at work one day looking at the rain fall. I noticed across the street a lady and her son waiting for the bus. I took my umbrella out to her so she could stay a little dry at least. It was a five-dollar umbrella, so it was no big deal. But it was an opportunity to show kindness.

Now before you think me to be some saint or something,

I am not. There are times when I have been so distracted by work, family, and life that I have completely passed by a person in need. It would be an hour later, and all of a sudden, I would think, *Man, why didn't I stop for her or reach out to them?* Then I feel lousy for two days.

Opportunities are God's ways of keeping us connected to each other, meeting needs, and sharing the good news of Jesus Christ. We decide if we take the leap or hold back. Oftentimes distractions keep us from seeing and hearing opportunities God sends our way. Such opportunities could be a single mom crying for help with the kids or a pastor's cry for his sheep to listen and obey. It could be a coworker searching for the truth or a neighbor who needs a friend. Yet everyday events can distract us from responding to these needs, and opportunity slips away. We can train our hearts to see and hear nothing. Ouch! Did you hear that? We can train our hearts to see and hear nothing. Our hearts over time can become like a heavy rock, unmovable. Does it sound like one of our three characters?

David's men have now arrived and delivered David's message. They wait. Nabal now has the opportunity to respond. Does he take advantage of the opportunity given him to reach out and be kind, or does he let it slip away? Nabal's response is worth looking at clearly.

Then Nabal answered David's servants, and said, "Who is David, and who is the son of Jesse? There are many servants nowadays who break away each one from his master. Shall I then take my bread and my water and my meat that I have killed for my shearers, and give it to men when I do not know where they are from?"

Nabal's response is short, disrespectful, and selfish. Nabal has more than enough but refuses to share. There is no way he didn't know who David is. We later see Abigail, his wife, knows (1 Samuel 25:28–33). Nabal is living up to his profile, harsh. His own heart has condemned him. Nabal has been given the opportunity to help others and yet responds with no grace and harshness. His own selfish demeanor distracted him. Nabal lived for Nabal. The only opportunity he would take was for himself.

How often do we ourselves respond as Nabal did? I mean, we may not see ourselves as harsh and graceless as Nabal, but think about this. Our child comes through the den, and we are watching TV.

Our child says, "Play with me."

We respond, "Honey, I am so tired. I worked all day. Can we do this another time?"

See, opportunity slips away. We get distracted from what

God has for us as well. Kindness is not just for the person we show the kindness to; it is for our heart as well. Kindness, giving, and sharing all spring from a heart next to God's heart, which is all about love and kindness.

Look what He did on the cross and the sacrifice given, His only Son, Jesus. Yet we too complain or make excuses. We complain about giving yet fail to see the opportunity in helping spread the gospel to places we may never go. We complain about the music in church yet fail to see the young people who come to hear the Word because of that music. We get frustrated when someone calls for help on our day off yet fail to see the opportunity to help an unsaved neighbor. We do not have time to listen, call, or write.

Nabal refuses to be moved, so Jesus moves down the road to Calvary. Had He not, we would be lost. I wonder if Nabal knew if what were about to happen next would have changed his response. Maybe not. But one can only hope. The heart of this matter is the heart, and it matters.

Look for Opportunity

Go on a quest with me. For the next week, look for opportunities God sends your way. He will. He wants to. Listen to His still, small voice as He opens doors of opportunities to serve Him better. Of course, those opportunities can be huge; however, God often sends subtle or delicate opportunities to minister to others. You have to want to. You have to move. Pray and ask God to open doors and wait and see what He does.

Now remember we do have an enemy who is the king of missed opportunities. Satan will do everything in his power to distract us from the opportunities God has for us. And they are not all bad. It could be the difference of helping a friend or cleaning the house. If we don't like cleaning, well, there you have it. If we are not in good standing with that friend, the house sure needs cleaning. You get the idea.

Satan can cause distractions on top of distractions. Fix your eyes on Jesus, and you will begin to see the difference. Pray, study the Word, and then look, listen, and respond to God's Holy Spirit as He leads.

Opportunity and the Next Step

Sometimes opportunity will come, and we simply do not know how to begin. I have been there before. Don't throw in the towel. Look for resources. For example, a family in your church has been burned out of their home. They will need everything. Team up with your church, community Red Cross, Salvation Army, your city, and so forth to help this family.

Sometimes opportunity means working as a team, not just as an individual. I have the awesome privilege of working with Samaritans Purse and am a chaplain with the Billy Graham Rapid Response Team. We go into places hit with catastrophe and help the people as best we can. We repair homes, churches, and buildings as we share God's love and His gospel. Working as a team, we see God's marvelous work as we take advantage of the opportunity given to us. When opportunity knocks, open the door. Don't slam the door on opportunity as Nabal did. We will find out he made the wrong choice. God provides opportunity. We need only to take it.

Galatians 6:10

"Therefore, <u>as we have opportunity</u>, let us do good to all, especially to those who are of the household of faith."

Chapter 3

I Got This!

Anger is such a complex emotion. Some people are angry and forget or never know what made them angry. Anger can get us off track from the real issues. We can lose focus. And as a result, we may react to a situation using poor choices or judgment. Finding the root problem to one's anger is the key to unlocking the anger and moving beyond the struggle. Staying in the anger breeds a whole new batch of problems that result in more issues.

When David sent his men to ask Nabal for food, Nabal's reply was harsh and disrespectful. Nabal could have cared less how David felt. David's men return with Nabal's answer, and David's response is not pretty.

So David's young men turned on their heels and went back; and they came and told him all these words. Then David said to his men, "Every man gird on his sword." So, every man girded on his sword, and David also girded on his sword. And about four hundred men went with David, and two hundred stayed with the supplies. (1 Samuel 25:12–13)

Now where is David going, and what is he going to do? I will give you three guesses. Nabal's response has now caused a response in David. And he is angry.

For clarity, does Nabal's response make David's response right? "Be angry, and do not sin: do not let the sun go down on your wrath" (Ephesians 4:26). David had been disrespected, dealt with harshly, and made to look unimportant in front of his men. Yes, he is angry and rightly so.

However, David is about to take matters into his own hands. How do we know? The scripture tells us.

Now David had said, "Surely in vain I have protected all that this fellow has in the wilderness, so that nothing was missed of all that belongs to him. And he has repaid me evil for good. May God do so, and more also, to the enemies of David, if I leave one male

of all who belong to him by morning light."
(1 Samuel 25:21–22)

David is angry, and he is about to show Nabal just what happens when you cross him. It is important to note that not only is David headed for disaster, he is taking others with him as well. Remember those men who are following David (1 Samuel 22). They are right beside him. Uncontrolled anger always includes others. People may not have made that decision had they been given another choice.

Notice what God's Word says. "Be angry, and do not sin: do not let the sun go down on your wrath." Anger, if channeled right, can motivate us to do something. When I see another person mistreating people on the news, I want to help. I get angry at bullying. I do not tolerate it. I was traveling home one day and saw a crowd of young people with two girls in the center of this group. The crowd was pushing the girls into one another, yelling, "Hit her! Hit her!"

I jumped out of my car, ran over, and asked the girls to look around. They were entertainment for the crowd. It made me angry that all those people were trying to get those girls to hurt each other so they could be entertained. Anger can help us move to act and move in the right direction when channeled rightly. But it must be with the right motives and intentions. Anything less is wrong.

That same verse in Ephesians also says not to let the sun

go down while you are angry. Don't stew on what makes you angry. It's like a fire that won't go out. Someone will get burned for sure. Give yourself time to cool off and focus on what went wrong and find a calm solution. Get a mature third party involved if you have to.

Anger can be one of the biggest heart issues we face. It can destroy homes, families, and businesses and start wars. Untreated anger can cause great harm. When one is angry and it goes unresolved, it becomes like a simmering coal, and we tend to forget why we are angry. The facts get distorted and confused. The enemy Satan loves it when we remain angry at each other. Nothing is accomplished for the kingdom of God. Satan, the great instigator, loves to keep the fires burning. And he will help you keep it going and going till all is destroyed.

Remember there is only one who, when He is angry, is righteous and perfect. That would be our God. Jesus was in the temple, and He was angry because they had turned His house into a den of thieves (Matthew 21:12–13; Mark 11:15–17; Luke 19:46). Righteous anger is God. David is about to let his anger get the best of him. He would go into Nabal's camp and destroy every last male there. David is mad and angry, and his vision is becoming more distorted by the minute.

David had done nothing wrong to be treated so badly. However, as they say, two wrongs don't make a right. Taking things into your own hands, especially as a child of God, never works out. When unchecked anger gets the best of us, our hearts are not at their best.

I have been there before. Have you? Someone hurts my feeling or says something to me or about me, and I respond with angry words or actions. I am not waiting on God but thinking I can handle things better than He can by doing it myself. Do you see how things can get distorted and confused? Who in the world can even come close to almighty God? Yet anger undealt with makes us think our way is best.

Pray, Trust, and Think

Things do not always go as planned. We can become irritated, frustrated, or even angry. People are still people. What I mean by that is this: it does not matter if we are reading about the actions of Nabal in the book of Samuel or dealing with a person today. People have not changed that much. There is always going to be those who behave badly and those who get angry easily. You or I could be either. The fact is that people are people and can hurt or anger us at any time. Family, church family, coworkers, neighbors, or road warriors, the list is endless. We have to learn to deal with others of this nature in a godly, biblical manner to prevent the obvious, a possible catastrophe.

Nabal is an evil-dealing man. David is angry at his misdealings and his lack of respect. Neither one of these men is going to give an inch, and therein lies the problem. Someone has to rise above the issues and not be distracted by the circumstances. Yes, our feelings are hurt. Yes, I am angry. Yes, I want them to know how angry I am. However, without praying for the wisdom of God, thinking the situation through, or trusting the guidance of God's Holy Spirit in our lives, we could make a terrible rash decision. And when we take things into our own hands and bathe it with anger, it never goes well.

So what to do? Stop and pray. I know you are thinking, *that is way too simple.* Let me ask you: have you ever tried to pray when you are really angry? Be honest. What we start with is, "God, let them trip and knock some sense into their head." The last thing we want to do is pray blessings on them.

In 1 Samuel 12, the prophet Samuel was speaking to the people of Israel. They had decided that they needed a king. Samuel was upset with them because they already had the King of Kings as their king. Yet they had to have their king, which they received. I will let you read that story for yourself; however, Samuel warned them that even though they had a king, they should not be distracted from following God.

He followed this by saying that even though he was upset with them, he would continue to pray for them. Prayer is not a simple thing. It is a battlefield and where the fight begins. Prayer changes our circumstances. Prayer is powerful because of where prayer is directed, the Lord Jesus Christ. We realize in and of ourselves that we can do nothing.

When I am in a heated situation, Christ is the person I run to. He calms my heart. When I first begin to pray, I may be angry or frustrated; however, as I unwind and yield in my prayer, Jesus provides the calm I need. The solution may take time, but I can now in the presence of Christ stay focused and find that needed solution.

Trust the Lord as you seek Him out to guide you in a right choice for you and the other person or persons. Trust the Father to guide you as only He can. Trust the Lord to pull away the curtain of your heart to reveal what is hindering healing. Anger unchecked leads to a distorted view of the facts and can distract us from the truth and solution. It doesn't matter how the other person responds. That is God's territory. Our focus is on our right walk with the Lord.

Second, seek out a spiritually mature person to help you stay focused. Why spiritually mature? First, you need someone who studies the scripture and knows how God would have you respond. We all have an opinion, and we all think we are right. But if that opinion is not in line with the Word of God, we may get unwise council. God's Word does not change; His Word is true from cover to cover.

When you study the Word daily, you will see God's heart and what He says about how we treat each other. A person who is a disciple of the Word and sticks with the Word of God will use God's Word as his or her measuring stick to guide and instruct. Samuel knew this. The judges and prophets of the Old Testament knew what God said, and they guided God's people by His truth, not their own. That person can help us make the right choice by sharing God's Word.

Having the gift of encouragement, I have developed a letter ministry over the years and have counted this ministry a joy and privilege in encouraging others. Even though I send words of encouragement, I mostly love to send the Word of God because His words say so much more than I ever could. When you find yourself in a situation of this sort, pray, trust, and think first. Let us grab hold of ourselves before Satan does. His Word says it all!

Proverbs 3:5–6

"Trust in the Lord with all your heart, And lean not on your own understanding; In all your ways acknowledge Him, And He shall direct your paths."

Chapter 4

Prerogative

Prerogative, according to the Cambridge dictionary, means "a special advantage that allows some people the freedom to do or have something that is not possible or allowed for everyone."[2]

Okay? Why start here? We as a people sometimes think we have the right to act any old way we want. This could be the most difficult yet most important chapter in this book. We hear this all the time: "I am entitled … It is my prerogative to do this … It is my choice to do this or that or to say what I think." If everyone practices this way of thinking, we are in big trouble.

---

[2] "Prerogative," https://dictionary.cambridge.org/us/dictionary/english/prerogative.

Let's face it. If I said everything that came into my head, well, let's just say it would not be pretty. Having the attitude that I can say or do what I want is faulty thinking. When David sent his young men to approach Nabal in 1 Samuel 25:2–42, Nabal was less than gracious and quite rude. Nabal gave no thought to his words and wasn't about to give David or his men anything. Nabal certainly had a choice to refuse David food. It was his food. And certainly, Nabal had a choice to behave the way he did. However, at what cost?

> Now David had said, "Surely in vain I have protected all that this fellow has in the wilderness, so that nothing was missed of all that belongs to him. And he has repaid me evil for good. May God do so, and more also, to the enemies of David, if I leave one male of all who belong to him by morning light." (1 Samuel 25:21–22)

As mentioned before, Nabal was not a nice guy who did not mince words. David, on the other hand, had been kind to Nabal's men and even kept them from harm while they were in the field. David was polite and respectful. Unfortunately, Nabal used his prerogative to behave badly. Look at this example nearly everyone can relate too.

You are in traffic, and this person cuts you off. You slam

on the brakes. Man, you could just run over the guy. Or perhaps you are getting ready to pull into a parking space, and someone shoots in front of you. I once watched a video where someone did just that, and when the person went inside, the other guy pulled the car out and left their car sitting in the middle of the road.

Yes, we do have the choices. We can say and do what we want, but should we? Is this what the scripture teaches? No, not at all.

> Jesus said to him, "You shall love the Lord your God with all your heart, with all your soul, and with all your mind." This is the first and great commandment. And the second is like it: "You shall love your neighbor as yourself." On these two commandments hang all the Law and the Prophets. (Matthew 22:37–40)

These verses say it all. I would dare say Nabal somehow missed this. And David is about to throw it to the wind. We see the condition of Nabal's heart and the heart of David changing. As Christians, we love our God, and we want to love each other. But let's face it: it can be hard. I am quite sure I may have acted no differently than David in this situation. I may not have climbed on a horse and took off to wipe out his menfolk, but I may have killed Nabal in my heart. And we have all done that at some point.

Stay with me. You know the drill. Someone hurts you. Boom! You now can no longer speak to that person, at least in a polite manner. We want them to know our hurt and will spare no expense in letting them know. We will slowly kill them with silence, words, innuendos, and the such. Are you following me? We may not literally use a sword, but we may utilize other tools Satan gives us to kill someone emotionally or spiritually. Satan has a whole toolbox of tools he would love to give you.

I once heard a man say the only tool Satan has in his toolbox is our sins. Yes, and those sins can get us in all kinds of trouble if we choose them. Satan has a toolbox full and is ready to give those tools to you any time you want them—like pride, resentment, hostility, and anger. And the list goes on. You see that entitlement, self, and pride cover the toolbox. To our distorted vision, it looks good. We have to reach into the toolbox and take those tools out before they have power over us. It is our choice.

There is a reason Jesus wanted us to love God first and then each other. If our focus is on God, we will want to do the right thing, even when we are hurt. But if we let the wounds of our hearts blind us, we will not love others as ourselves. We will become the one who does the hurting. No longer focused on God and His truths, we are distracted by the lies of Satan, and we have the prerogative to do or say what we want.

Both Nabal and David feel this way. "He insulted me. Now I will get him back." Where does it end? Someone must be willing to put self aside, listen to the voice of truth, and allow God's wisdom to work its way into our hearts. This way we will not become the offender.

Don't Be Distracted by Self

Nabal frankly was a mess and didn't know it. He said and did whatever he wanted. He gave no thought to others. I mean, he started out and ended that way.

How about us? Where do we stand? Do we feel entitled all the time? Do we get offended easily because perhaps the preacher didn't speak to us today? Maybe your grown child didn't call this week. Perhaps you feel because you have suffered through a difficult situation you have a right to be grumpy.

I have celiac disease.[3] It can be painful at times. Sometimes staying locked up in the house and remaining in bed seems like the best thing to do. Being in pain a lot can make you grumpy. But I have the choice to be a grump or ask Jesus to help me be an overcomer.

---

[3] "What Is Celiac Disease?" https://celiac.org/celiac-disease/understanding-celiac-disease-2/what-is-celiac-disease.

I prefer to be an overcomer. I quite frankly find myself praying some days for extra strength to be kind. I feel bad saying that, but when you hurt all the time, whether in your body or your heart, it is tough. I want to be kind, serve my God, and be the best encourager I can be. Don't you think it is funny that God would choose to give me the gift of encouragement living with this disease?

What about you? Do you have an attitude that you are owed or you have the prerogative to do or say what you feel? Do you feel offended easily or somehow you are the victim all the time? I don't mean to step on toes, but these attitudes are not of God. Being mean and hurtful does not glorify God. Nabal represents those who feel they can do as they please, and if you don't like it, too bad. David, on the other hand, represents those who want to be kind, considerate, and Christ-like but somehow get distracted by the hurts and pains of this world. Those distractions can lead you down a road of chaos, if not checked. What to do?

First, don't be a Nabal. He had it all wrong. He thought he had the prerogative to do or say what he pleased. God has another plan. Take some time right now to examine your heart. Is it stone, becoming stone, or yearning to please God? David got distracted for a time, but we will see that David yearned to do the right thing. The time you take to seek God's face will be the best time you have spent all week.

Matthew 7:7 reads, "<u>Ask</u>, and it will be given to you; <u>seek</u>, and you will find; <u>knock</u>, and it will be opened to you."

Second, when you find yourself in the same place David found himself, don't respond with vengeance, malice, or unkindness. Take that person and the situation to God and let Him handle it. He will in His time and in the right place.

When I was a young woman working in the workforce, I got accused of something I did not do. I was a new Christian, and I could not understand how I could be treated that way. I was so hurt that I could just die. But I knew God saw all things and trusted Him with the situation. Twenty years later, the man who accused me sought me out because he too had become a Christian and wanted to apologize for the accusations. Now that is the power of God.

It may seem a long time, but God's timing is not like ours. And yes, we hugged, and all was forgiven. God is so good. Things may not always turn out this way, and many, for me, have not; however, with God in control, it will turn out for the best. Don't let the circumstances distract you from doing what God would have you do. Ask, seek, and knock. He'll answer.

Hebrews 12:1–3

"Therefore we also, since we are surrounded by so great a cloud of witnesses, let us lay aside every weight, and the sin which so easily ensnares us, and let us run with endurance the race that is set before us, <u>looking unto Jesus,</u> the author and finisher of our faith, who for the joy that was set before Him endured the cross, despising the shame, and has sat down at the right hand of the throne of God."

Toni S. Troxell

Chapter 5

A Focused Heart

Have you ever noticed how easily we can get distracted in life? I mean, take an untrained hound dog in the woods, and after the first squirrel, he is gone. Another example is that project in the garage. You start cleaning out boxes, and you come across that package with all the good stuff in it. You know the one that has all those pictures you took on vacation or those items from when the kids were small. Perhaps it's from those high school days. We sit down and go through all those pictures, going, "Aww, I forgot this one."

All of a sudden two hours later, the garage is not cleaned, and you have run out of time. It's no big deal. You can do it another day. Unfortunately, another day may be next summer. Staying focused on the task at hand can be bit of a challenge at times. Being focused to the task takes discipline. You tell your child to clean their room, and they will get distracted and end up playing with the dolls, trucks, or, in some cases, video games.

Our walk with the Lord is no different. We get distracted. Through everyday events, what lies in our hearts will be revealed. There's no time to study the scripture because the house needs cleaning or you have laundry to do. There's no time to pray. The grass needs mowed, or the car needs an oil change. You say, "I'll get to it when I get the time." About church, one may assert, "I don't go to church. It is my only day off." Or for tithing, he may relate, "I can barely eat now." And the list goes on.

When an issue comes along that demands our attention, we can make all kinds of excuses and let distractions have their way. However, we put off some things could be extremely costly, for example, spending time with family. Tomorrow is not another day. In 1 Samuel, we have seen Nabal's harshness. We have seen the future king of Israel, David, show kindness to Nabal, only to be disrespected.

Now David seeks revenge and is on his way with quite a few men to follow through with his plans. The heart of both men is now exposed—revenge and harshness. Self has become the major issue, and when this happens, life is not a party. It's chaos. Pride and selfishness are like putting on a pair of glasses with black lens. You are bound to hit a brick wall. Keeping our eyes focused on God's heart through His Word can be the greatest preventer of such problems as pride and self. Focused and calm is not where David and Nabal have landed.

However, in the center of all these emotions, Abigail enters the picture. 1 Samuel 25:3 reads, "The name of the man was Nabal, and the name of his wife Abigail. And she was a woman of good understanding and beautiful appearance." Not only is Abigail beautiful, she is wise. Wow! What a combination! She is respected in her home and among her servants. At some point Abigail had demonstrated the fact she was a wise woman. The servants of Abigail and Nabal come to Abigail with the news that trouble is coming.

> Now one of the young men told Abigail, Nabal's wife, saying, "Look, David sent messengers from the wilderness to greet our master; and he reviled them. But the men were very good to us, and we were not hurt, nor did we miss anything as long as we accompanied them, when we were in the fields. They were a wall to us both by night and day, all the time we were with them keeping the sheep. Now therefore, know and consider what you will do, for harm is determined against our master

and against all his household. For he is such a scoundrel that one cannot speak to him." (1 Samuel 25:14–17)

Can you imagine what Abigail must have thought? She obviously knows her husband. The Bible does not paint a beautiful picture of Nabal or cast him in a good light. On the contrary, it says, "The servant said of Nabal, 'he is such a scoundrel that one cannot speak to him ...'" (verse 17). In other words, he is not a nice person, and to top it off, there is no reasoning with him. Nabal is just a difficult person.

Is there anybody in your life like that? The scripture does not give much detail into Abigail's reactions or emotions; however, we see she realized the severity of the problem. As we will see, she is focused on solving the problem. Abigail's heart would take on the appearance of grace and wisdom.

There is a great song out right now by Danny Gokey called "Haven't Seen It Yet," and in that song, a great line says, "He had the solution before you had the problem."[4] I love that line. How differently we would see our circumstances if we realized God knows what you are going through and He already knows how He is going to resolve every issue. Although the scripture does not say Abigail prayed, I

---

[4] C. Wedgeworth, and E. Hulse, "Danny Gokey-Haven't Seen It Yet Lyrics," https://lyricsfa.com/2019/01/12/danny-gokey-havent-seen-it-yet-lyrics.

believe she did. The Bible describes Abigail as a woman of good "understanding" (verse 3). And understanding comes from God.

Remember Nebuchadnezzar in the Old Testament. He made this statement after pride got into his heart and God humbled him. Daniel 4:34 reads, "And at the end of the time I, Nebuchadnezzar, lifted my eyes to heaven, and my understanding returned to me; and I blessed the Most High and praised and honored Him who lives forever: For His dominion is an everlasting dominion, And His kingdom is from generation to generation."

God gives wisdom, understanding, and discernment. God provides us the understanding to handle every problem if we will listen to Him, follow Him, and wait on Him (if necessary) and the discernment to know the difference. Abigail understands what needs to happen next by her understanding, which comes from God, and she wastes no time moving. Now the plot not only thickens, it gets downright muddy.

So here is the problem. Nabal is difficult. David comes and makes a request, and Nabal makes the terrible choice to disrespect David. (Understanding and wisdom went right out the door.) Now David is on his way to get his revenge. At this point, the situation seems very frightening. I am sure everyone, except Nabal, is in a state of panic.

Now the servant comes to make Abigail aware of the

problem. This servant must have seen Abigail in action before because he seemed to know that she will do something. What a person of character! What a heart! Abigail does not disappoint. She jumps right in there with both feet. There is no time to be filled with fear and panic. She understands the situation and responds with wisdom, grace, humility, and bravery, and her heart is focused. She has to respond and move.

I am often amazed at the bravery of those in the military or first responders. When they arrive on a scene, they are focused. There can be all kinds of distractions going on, yet they are so focused. And aren't we glad! If you have ever needed this kind of help, you know you can depend on them to do what it takes to get and keep you safe. Soap box time: I will never understand why we attack our police officers or firefighters or those who seek our best interest. They do so much to help us. Trust me, if you ever find yourself in a violent situation, you will be glad they are there. I appreciate all they and others in their field do for us.

Abigail is on the move.

> Then Abigail made haste and took two hundred loaves of bread, two skins of wine, five sheep already dressed, five seahs of roasted grain, one hundred clusters of raisins, and two hundred cakes of figs, and loaded them on donkeys. And

she said to her servants, "Go on before me; see, I am coming after you." But she did not tell her husband Nabal. (1 Samuel 25:18–19)

That is a lot of food. Notice in verse 18 that the scripture says, "Abigail made haste." David is coming, and he is mad. Her family and servants depend on her to be focused. They know her heart and trust her to do the right thing. To delay may be too late or worse. When we are given a task, do we give it our all? "And whatever you do, do it heartily, as to the Lord and not to men" (Colossians 3:23).

When we serve the Lord, when God gives us a task, is it done as if we are doing it for our Lord? It somewhat puts a different spin on things. When we serve the Lord, we are to focus on the service in front of us and do it to the best of our ability, no matter what. When we serve the Lord, it takes heart. Look at the heart of Jesus, who went all the way to the cross and finished the work set before Him. Aren't we glad He finished the work?

Abigail knows her family and servants are counting on her. If she loses focus, all might be lost. Abigail moves quickly to head off the disaster. She packs a lot of food, sends her servant ahead, and tells him that she is on her way. An interesting fact here is that Abigail could have sent her servant alone and not go herself. She could have just stayed home. That would have been the easy thing to do.

But Abigail knows it would take more than a lot of food to correct this problem. As the woman of the house, she feels responsible for what goes on there. How refreshing! In our world today, people struggle to take responsibility for their own actions, much less the poor actions of another. We feel it is so much easier to pass the buck. Abigail uses wisdom and practices humility to solve the issue. Even though Nabal had made the mess, she does not include him in the plans. You can imagine what he would have said or done, and the problem would have ended in bloodshed.

Do let me share this: the focus we put on our walk with the Lord speaks volumes to those around us, our families, neighbors, coworkers, and church family. It says to others how we view God and how we trust in Him. When we are distracted from our walk with God, those around us begin to notice, and they too may get distracted in their walk.

Take our children, for example. What we focus on, they will focus on. What we deem important, they will. How can we send our children into the world laced with so many distractions without God and Christ as the number-one priority? What a tragedy! Staying focused on God and the task at hand will prove to be the best blessing we could ever give those around us.

Abigail is now on her way into a very troubling situation. She has no idea what would happen. I can only imagine how she must have felt at this point and in the moments ahead where she would face David. Abigail has her husband behind her being himself and David and four hundred men in front of her on a mission to take lives. She must remain focused to the task and leave the results to God.

When we are faced with life-altering changes and choices, we must trust the Lord. There is no other way. We can't know the future. We have no idea what tomorrow will bring. But our God does. And come what may, God is in control. What a peace and calm this can bring. Here she goes.

> So it was, as she rode on the donkey, that she went down under cover of the hill; and there were David and his men, coming down toward her, and she met them. Now David had said, "Surely in vain I have protected all that this fellow has in the wilderness, so that nothing was missed of all that belongs to him. And he has repaid me evil for good. May God do so, and more also, to the enemies of David, if I leave one male of all who belong to him by morning light." (1 Samuel 25:20–22)

Abigail focuses and goes to meet David and his men. Abigail has no idea what response to expect. She knows David's mission; however, she has a mission of her own. Can you see the wheels turning in her head? Her focus is on an outcome that would protect those in her household, and that would be Nabal as well.

How Focused Are You?

When it comes to your walk with the Lord, on a scale of one to ten, where are you? A one is great; a ten is not so great. (And yes, I meant it that way.) If you are a one, awesome! However, many of us are not. If you are a ten, let's work on that. Here are three simple ways to focus your walk on the Lord:

1. Go to Bible study. Start a devotional time every single day. I get up at 3:00 a.m. every morning before work. I need this time with my Lord. Nothing else can take this place. I mostly use "Turning Point" with Dr. David Jeremiah and still some others. Studying God's Word is one of the most important disciplines a Christian can develop.
2. Pray. Sometimes I pray first; other times I pray after my Bible study. As we read the Word of God, He speaks to us. As we pray, we speak to Him, and the communication is ongoing, as it should be.
3. Fellowship with other believers. Belonging to a Bible-believing and Bible-teaching church is very important. We encourage each other as we walk daily with our

Lord. But keep in mind, if the Lord Jesus Christ is not your Lord and Savior, none of these things matter. We are all sinners and in need of a Savior, Jesus Christ. In the back of this book, you will find details about salvation in Christ Jesus.

Psalm 34:8

"Oh, taste and see that the Lord is good; Blessed is the man who trusts in Him!"

Chapter 6

The Heart Unseen

T he heart! Who can know it, right? God does! "So God, who knows the heart, acknowledged them by giving them the Holy Spirit, just as He did to us" (Acts 15:8). We find Nabal's heart revealed in the scripture, "but the man (Nabal) was harsh and evil in his doings" (1 Samuel 25:3).

Nabal put his heart out there for all to see, and pretty it is not. Yet Abigail, his wife, is seen in a different light. "And she was a woman of good understanding and beautiful appearance" (1 Samuel 25:3). We only get a peek into the hearts of Nabal, David, and Abigail. So much we do not know. Evidently some people thought Nabal was okay because they celebrated with him, right? (1 Samuel 25:11, 36). Or were they just like-minded?

David's men followed him and were ready to do whatever he said, even if innocent people may die (1 Samuel 25:13). They trusted his judgment and heart. The servants of Abigail sought her out when trouble came because they knew her heart and trusted her wisdom (1 Samuel 25:14–17).

In each situation, Nabal, David, and Abigail has revealed a piece of themselves, which lets us get a momentary glimpse into their heart. You and I do not see all the details that are in the hearts of others, but God observes every detail. Sometimes when we look at each other, we can form an opinion without ever knowing the heart of an individual.

The heart, the real person, is a complex place in most people. Lots of stuff can go on in there. Yet for God, there is no mystery about us at all. When no one seems to get us, God does. When we feel invisible, God sees. When no one seems to hear our concerns, God does. When David was chosen as the future king, all his brothers were seen first. They were older and more experienced, yet God told Samuel, "Do not look at his appearance or at his physical stature, because I have refused him. For the Lord does not see as man sees; for man looks at the outward appearance, but the Lord looks at the heart" (1 Samuel 16:7).

No one that day even thought of David as king. Yet God looks at our heart. Nabal, Abigail, and David were no secret to the God of all creation, and neither are we. No matter how invisible we may think we are or try to be, God sees all.

Nothing escapes Him. That is why we can trust Him with the details as well as the results.

Abigail is on her way to meet David, and she is trusting God. She speaks not only to the heart of David but about the heart of her husband. There's no glamour, just truth.

> Now when Abigail saw David, she dismounted quickly from the donkey, fell on her face before David, and bowed down to the ground. So she fell at his feet and said: "On me, my lord, on me let this iniquity be! And please let your maidservant speak in your ears and hear the words of your maidservant. Please, let not my lord regard this scoundrel Nabal. For as his name is, so is he: Nabal is his name, and folly is with him! But I, your maidservant, did not see the young men of my lord whom you sent." (1 Samuel 25:23–25)

Abigail gets right to the point. She tells the truth about Nabal. He is a "scoundrel." She takes the blame, and she has no idea that David's men had paid a visit. There are no excuses, just truth and humility. How awesome is that! I do not know if I would have done all that for someone who was not so nice. Yet this is the theme of the gospel. When we were still sinners, Christ died for us (Romans 5:8).

We were not lovely people. We did not have it all together. We are sinners. Abigail could have let the chips fall where they may and let Nabal get what he deserved. Who would have blamed her? After all, he was not a nice guy. Why worry about David and what he would do?

Yet here she is face down in the dirt, asking for David to forgive her and hear her out. In times of deepest struggles and troubles, a person's heart is often revealed. Some are brave; others are not so brave. A few are weak; some are strong. A handful are good; others are not so good.

Yet the beautiful picture in all of this is that Christ came to die for all of us, every heart. No matter what goes on in there, God loves each of us. He loves the Nabals of the world as much as the Abigails and the Davids. That means you and me. Sometimes I feel like my heart is invisible to others. Good and bad, I keep it hid at times. Yet we are told to bear one another's burdens (Galatians 6:2; Ephesians 4:2; Colossians 3:13).

Abigail put into practice this principle as she approached David. She has the weight of her whole household and family on her shoulders because of one simple act her husband had thoughtlessly performed. Her heart is revealed in the actions she performs that one day. Never mind there are four hundred men surrounding her (1 Samuel 25:13) and a soon-to-be king who is angry. Never mind she has a husband at home she could not reason with (1 Samuel 25:17).

Her heart is set on the task at hand, to save lives. Abigail's mission is to be a peace maker. Her heart is set on peace and the safety of her family. Abigail cares about the decision David is about to make as she reminds David of his mission and whom he is.

> Now therefore, my lord, as the Lord lives and as your soul lives, since the Lord has held you back from coming to bloodshed and from avenging yourself with your own hand, now then, let your enemies and those who seek harm for my lord be as Nabal. And now this present which your maidservant has brought to my lord, let it be given to the young men who follow my lord. Please forgive the trespass of your maidservant. For the Lord will certainly make for my lord an enduring house, because my lord fights the battles of the Lord, and evil is not found in you throughout your days. Yet a man has risen to pursue you and seek your life, but the life of my lord shall be bound in the bundle of the living with the Lord your God; and the lives of your enemies He shall sling out, as from the pocket of a sling. And it shall come to pass, when the Lord has done for my lord according to all the good that He has spoken concerning you, and has appointed you ruler over Israel, that this

will be no grief to you, nor offense of heart to my lord, either that you have shed blood without cause, or that my lord has avenged himself. But when the Lord has dealt well with my lord, then remember your maidservant. (1 Samuel 25:26–31)

Nabal claimed he had no idea whom David was (1 Samuel 25:10–11), yet Abigail seems to know quite a bit. It is just another layer pulled back from Nabal's heart. Picture Abigail face-to-face with the future king of Israel, the man she had heard so much about. Suppose he had a heart like Nabal? Would the problem only get worse?

When I talk to someone or hear about a difficulty for them, I try to put myself in their shoes. I may never have walked as Abigail, but I can imagine she had quite a bit of emotions running through her body. As Abigail speaks to David, she is reminding him "the Lord lives" and "evil is not found in you throughout your days" (1 Samuel 25:26, 28).

Abigail seems to be saying to David, "As God lives, He sees what happens. David, you have a good heart. Don't let these who pursue you and those like Nabal destroy that. God sees what has happened, and He'll take care of everything. Just don't do this thing that you are about to do. Two wrongs do not make a right." Abigail is trying to get David to look inside his heart and remember whom he belongs too and what his mission is, and that does not include wiping out innocent people in anger.

You have heard the following expressions, "have a heart" and "the heart of the matter." God says it this way, "Keep your heart with all diligence, For out of it spring the issues of life" (Proverbs 4:23). God's Word always says it better. Watch your heart. What comes out is already in there.

What's going on in your heart right now? Do you feel invisible? Are there issues undealt with? Have you forgotten whose child you are, if you are saved by the blood of Christ? Are you without the saving power of Christ's sacrifice on the cross, therefore confused about your heart issues? Let this chapter help you see the happenings of your heart.

Abigail has the ministry of remembering going on. She is helping David to see past the current circumstances and focus his heart on the living God who controls all things. Abigail is helping David remember that God has a future for him and he is a person of integrity. In the heat of the moment, David has forgotten whom he is and all those who looked to him. Abigail knows from what she had heard that David has a heart for God and for a moment ha forgotten that.

My heart and yours too is about my Lord and pleasing Him, yet sometimes I forget whom I belong to. I let foreign waste in my heart and end up following another way, sometimes causing havoc along the way. God always uses reminders to lead my heart back to Him. Abigail is a reminder to David from God of where his heart is and where it should be.

Guard Your Heart and the Hearts of Others

"Be anxious for nothing, but in everything by prayer and supplication, with thanksgiving, let your requests be made known to God; and the peace of God, which surpasses all understanding, <u>will guard your hearts</u> and minds through Christ Jesus" (Philippians 4:6–7).

When we read these verses, we associate them with prayer. And this is true and important. But one important fact is that when we give our concerns to God and are thankful, He will give us peace and guard our hearts and minds through Christ Jesus. Guard or watch over our hearts and minds.

I don't know about you, but I need God's help to guard my heart, thoughts, and mind. I want what comes out of my heart to be lovely and sweet to my heavenly Father, don't you? Listen to what comes out of your heart. You can tell by what comes out of your mouth and attitudes. Nabal gave no thought to his words, and we see where that is going. Abigail used the ministry of remembering to set David's heart back on track with God. When we are faced with the same issues as Abigail, this is what we can do:

1. Stop putting junk in your mind (what you read, listen to, or watch).
2. Study the scripture.
3. Pray and count your blessings daily.
4. Fight for your heart/guard your heart and use the ministry of remembering to help others and yourself to stay in right fellowship with God. Remember the goodness of God and the fellowship of His Word.

Psalm 51:10

"Create in me a clean heart, O God, and renew a steadfast spirit within me."

Chapter 7

Listen ... Listen ... Listen

A s we read in the last chapter, Abigail has given David much to think about. Using the ministry of remembering, Abigail has reminded David of who he is and who he is to become. Now David needs to listen, hear, and heed. Listening and hearing is a dying art. People are dying to be heard. The art of listening is just that, an art. It's a tool that has to be developed. Some get it; others don't.

I spoke of the ministry of remembering and now the ministry of listening. Why ministry? Like remembering, listening can change a person from doing the wrong thing and having the wrong response to making better and wiser choices. When someone helps us call to memory the goodness of God or the blessings on our life, we may rethink our current path. When I feel the need to complain about the current events, a gentle reminder of things God has delivered me from helps me put things into a better perspective.

So, it is with the ministry of listening. When we choose to listen to another, we place value on them. We say you matter. Abigail has no idea if David would listen, but that does not stop her from reaching out to him anyway. What she has to share with David is a matter of importance, and if unheard, it would be a matter of life and death. Not all messages may be this dramatic; however, to the speaker they are just as important. As a teacher of God's Word, I know how important it is that all people receive God's Word in their ear. Some want to hear, but others not so much.

Look at David for a moment. This is the picture he sees: a woman out of nowhere falls at his feet. She, a beautiful woman, is headfirst in the dirt. She keeps saying she is to blame. She has donkeys full of food. She is pleading her case in a humble and respectful manor. Even though he may not know her, she knows him. She seems to know all about him. And to top it off, this is the wife of the guy he is about to wipe out.

And how does David know all this? He's willing to stop and listen. Had he ridden on by, her things probably would have been a lot different. Abigail begins to explain, and David listens. Let me ask this question, and it may not be popular. When you text, who listens? What I mean is, how do you determine the tones and emotions of the person texting? So many times, a text message can be misinterpreted because the elements are not there.

As an employer, I do not like getting texts. Why? If I do not know the person very well, a text can be misleading to the meaning intended, and I have seen this many times. Abigail was there in the moment, and so was David. Don't get me wrong. A text is great to say "I will be late coming home" or a simple "love you," but there are times when being right there to hear and listen to someone is much more appropriate.

David could hear the heart of Abigail as he watches her actions and hears her voice. David could hear Abigail's concerns that David, in his anger, had perhaps forgotten. David listens and responds,

> "Blessed is the Lord God of Israel, who sent you this day to meet me! And blessed is your advice and blessed are you, because you have kept me this day from coming to bloodshed and from avenging myself with my own hand. For indeed, as the Lord God of Israel lives, who has kept me back from hurting you, unless you had hurried and come to meet me, surely by morning light no males would have been left to Nabal!" So David received from her hand what

she had brought him, and said to her, "Go up in peace to your house. See, I have heeded your voice and respected your person." (1 Samuel 25:32–35)

David listens and hears Abigail's wisdom. David does not remain in his anger or on his current path, but he moves to a place of humbleness himself. David, by listening, recognizes the voice of God through Abigail. By listening, David sees the ugly picture of destruction that was about to play out because of his anger. By listening, David turns away from his will to the awesomeness of God's will. David listens and is delivered from destruction and delivered to a place of peace. David realizes God is sending him a message through Abigail, and David stops on his path to follow God on His.

Isn't it so amazing how the ministry of listening can change everything? Nabal would not listen, and what a mess he created. Abigail listened to her servant who had an urgent message, and she leaped into action. David was on a path, a journey to avenge his name; however, by listening, his path was changed.

Along with listening, there is also hearing. I used to have a relative who was hard of hearing. Whenever you explained anything to him, you had to be deliberate and loud with your words, or he would almost always misunderstand what you said. Instead of "squirrels in the back," he heard "squirrels attack." Listening is important, yet getting the right message when you listen is just as important. Sometimes words fail me while trying to express what my heart is saying. Sometimes people may need a listening ear; however, they may also need an ear that hears correctly.

When listening to someone sometimes, I may find myself asking questions like, "So what you are saying is ..." I want to make sure I heard correctly. Without this element, people feel misunderstood. David practices this element of listening and hearing.

> Then David said to Abigail: "Blessed is the Lord God of Israel, who sent you this day to meet me! And blessed is your advice and blessed are you, <u>because you have kept me this day from coming to bloodshed and from avenging myself with my own hand.</u>" (1 Samuel 25:32–33)

David has listened to what Abigail had said. He finds no malice in her words or anything insulting. What he hears is a woman trying to help him make the right choice and that God is behind the message.

Sometimes people will share with me a bit of wisdom I may not be willing to hear. This is truly my loss. Listening and hearing go hand in hand. Whether a person needs to be heard or an individual need to listen, without hearing and listening it can be fruitless. Our response to what is heard can change our world.

David is a good listener. Although he is a little off the path, he hears the voice of God through the words of Abigail and responds with humble obedience. "So David received from her hand what she had brought him, and said to her, 'Go up in peace to your house. See, <u>I have heeded your voice</u> and respected your person'" (1 Samuel 25:35). David not only listened, he heard.

When I was a little girl, we played outside all day in the summertime till it got dark. I would listen for my mom's voice to say, "Come in the house. It's dark." Once I heard it though, I would keep playing till my mom would call again with even more authority. This time my mom would say, "Did you not hear me calling you? Were you not listening when I called?" It is a great thing to listen, but we do have to hear the message as well.

Listen and Hear!

In your own life right now, are you listening and hearing those around you? Do you feel heard? The Bible says He listens to our cries. He listens when we pray. It is not enough to listen; we must hear as well. Begin today to be a good listener. And when you listen, hear as well. Let it move you to the action that may be needed. God rejoices over you. God hears your heart.

Zephaniah 3:17 says, "The Lord your God in your midst, The Mighty One, will save; He will rejoice over you with gladness, He will quiet you with His love, He will rejoice over you with singing."

Proverbs 1:5

"A wise man will hear and increase learning, and a man of understanding will attain wise counsel, and hears our call."

Chapter 8

The Sovereignty of God

G od knows and controls all things—past, present, and future. Do you believe that, or does your actions say otherwise? How we view God and what we believe about Him determines how we see God and how we respond to Him. I truly believe that God is all powerful and knows all things, and I believe every word of the Bible. God is who He says He is—Creator God, All Present Father, Righteous and Holy God, the Giver of our Lord and Savior Jesus Christ. How we view God is revealed oftentimes in how we live and treat others. How we see God is seen in our hearts.

Abigail and David are both targets of Nabal's actions, Abigail by the fact he is her husband and David by way of insults. Both could have allowed themselves to become victims; however, we see in the scripture that they followed the plan of God, and as a result they were the victors in the end. They go from victim to victor by allowing God to guide them instead of going their own way.

No matter where you go, no matter what you do, there will always be those who do whatever they like at others' expense. Some feel they are entitled and resort to stealing and hurting others. Like Nabal, we can take the road of insult to injury (literally in his case) or take the road of Abigail and David. We do get to choose. Being a child of God does not mean, "I no longer have a will or mind of my own." I choose to yield to God. David and Abigail yielded; Nabal did not. David listened to Abigail and turned away from the destructive path he was on. Abigail was spared death and havoc on her home and family. Nabal did not walk away so fortunate.

> Now Abigail went to Nabal, and there he was, holding a feast in his house, like the feast of a king. And Nabal's heart was merry within him, for he was very drunk; therefore she told him nothing, little or much, until morning light. So it was, in the morning, when the wine had gone from Nabal, and his wife had told him these things, that his heart died within him, and he became like a stone. Then it happened, after

about ten days, that the Lord struck Nabal, and he died. (1 Samuel 25:36–38)

Sobering, isn't it? Nabal thought he had it all and he could do it all and act any oh way. God is faithful and slow to anger. "The Lord is slow to anger and great in power And will not at all acquit the wicked. The Lord has His way In the whirlwind and in the storm, And the clouds are the dust of His feet" (Nahum 1:3). Yet we fail to understand God. He is holy. "Exalt the Lord our God, And worship at His holy hill; For the Lord our God is holy" (Psalm 99:9).

The fear of the Lord is fading, and people actually feel as if God cannot see or hear their sins. This is a bad place to be. Before I became a Christian, I thought Christians were not the people I wanted to hang out with. Even after Jesus saved me, adjusting to living a life guided by the Word of God took time. This God understands. I am a person in the process of finishing. How about you?

However, those who deliberately turn away from God or scoff at His Word will deal with Him. God alone knows every heart, and for that I am grateful. We cannot judge another's heart; we have to leave that to God and let Him sort it all out. Abigail reacted in a positive way to a negative situation, with no disrespect and no harshness. She responded in humility and submission. David, however, was on a path to handle the problem himself. God sent Abigail ahead to steer him right.

In the meantime, God dealt with Nabal. Abigail, David, or anyone else needed to confront Nabal. God took care of everything.

After David has taken what Abigail had brought, he sends her on her way in peace. When she arrives home, she finds Nabal in a drunken state and decides not to tell him at that time what had taken place. In the morning, Abigail waits till Nabal is sober and tells him all that had happened. Now what happens next is God at work. The reality of what could have happened bothered Nabal so bad the scripture says, "That his heart died within him, and he became like a stone" (1 Samuel 25:37).

Why this reaction? There could be a number of reasons. Matthew Henry's commentary notes that "he was ashamed of his own folly."[5] Could Nabal have been so disappointed in his actions that his heart turned like stone and he became unresponsive? The scripture does not say what this may mean nor the thoughts Nabal may have had, but one thing is for sure. It was more than he could handle. Imagine hearing the news that your own actions, yours alone, almost cost the lives of many people. For me that would be devastating.

Nabal had responded with rudeness and insults to David's request. Now the reality of those actions has hit home. After

---

[5] M. Henry, and L. F. Church, *Matthew Henry's Commentary in One Volume: Genesis to Revelation* (Grand Rapids: Zondervan Pub. House, 1999), 319.

ten days in this state, the scripture says, "Then it happened, after about ten days, that the Lord struck Nabal, and he died" (1 Samuel 25:38). The Lord took care of everything. God is in control. David, Abigail, all David's men, and Abigail's household has been spared. Nabal is now gone at the hand of the only true sovereign God.

This is a sober and solemn event. Nabal had no idea things would turn out this way. He just lived his life the way he wanted to. It did not seem to matter that his unchecked words and actions may injure others. As we see in the scripture, God had a better plan.

> So when David heard that Nabal was dead, he said, "Blessed be the Lord, who has pleaded the cause of my reproach from the hand of Nabal and has kept His servant from evil! For the Lord has returned the wickedness of Nabal on his own head." And David sent and proposed to Abigail, to take her as his wife. When the servants of David had come to Abigail at Carmel, they spoke to her saying, "David sent us to you, to ask you to become his wife." Then she arose, bowed her face to the earth, and said, "Here is your maidservant, a servant to wash the feet of the servants of my lord." So Abigail rose in haste and rode on a donkey, attended

by five of her maidens; and she followed the messengers of David, and became his wife. (1 Samuel 25:39–42)

God's plan is always greater than ours. When we feel that others hurt us, let God deal with the problem in His way and according to His timing. And understand if you think what you have planned or what you will say is better than God's, how terribly sad that is. God knows all things, and He takes care of His children. However, to take things into our own hands will only create more problems.

Turn It Over

As a manager of a retail store, I have worked with many different personalities, employees, and customers. When training a new employee, one of the first things I pass along is this: when a dissatisfied customer becomes upset, they are to walk away and come get me. The reason for this is that hopefully I will see things a little clearer and respond with a respectful solution. This allows the employee a way out of a possible sticky situation.

God handles our problems as well when we let Him. He is perfect and knows all things, and I do not. He can resolve any issue we have. His timing may be different and His ways not ours, but He can do anything. Trust and obey.

2 Samuel 22:31

"As for God, His way is perfect; The word of the Lord is proven; He is a shield to all who trust in Him."

Chapter 9

Don't Give Satan Room

I have no idea what condition your heart is in at this moment. If you are like me, there is stuff in there. The glorious fact is that even though I have stuff, Jesus still died for me. I am so humbled by this fact and wonderfully grateful. And I will one day be in glory with my Savior because of His grace and mercy. Till that day comes, I am here. You are here, and we need to be good soldiers guarding what He has given us, a heart for Him. And like any soldier, we have an enemy. And his goal is to keep us from being all God our Father meant us to be and to trip us up so our influence on others is nothing more than a fizzle instead of a fire. The devil is warring against us, and we have to stay close to God. Even though the battle is won, Satan can still have victories if we let him.

Think about this. Has anyone ever asked you these questions, "What's that look for? Don't use that tone with me! What's your problem?" (This is my least favorite.) Questions like these can take us off guard or even frustrate us. Perhaps inquiries such as these make us unsettled because someone may be getting a glimpse of our heart. The tones, attitudes, and motives we thought were hidden nicely away are not. There are places we have in our hearts that are off limits to others, places we even try to keep away from God, areas that are nicely tucked away out of view or so we think.

The curious thing is that there are times when we give the enemy permission to wander into our hearts as we try to keep God out. The Bible says, "Be angry, and do not sin: do not let the sun go down on your wrath, <u>nor give place to the devil</u>. Let him who stole steal no longer, but rather let him labor, working with his hands what is good, that he may have something to give him who has need" (Ephesians 4:26–28).

The heart is so delicate. This is why the scripture reminds us to guard our hearts. We are not to give Satan a place in our lives. All these things mentioned here—attitudes, motives, tones, words, and actions—can become a playground for the enemy if we let him. After a while the enemy will just come and stay. I am not talking about losing salvation here. Once Christ comes into our heart and saves us, we are saved. Nothing can snatch us from the Father's hands (John 10:29).

A Picture of Satan's Handiwork

Do you want to see a picture of giving Satan a place? I can give you a couple, for instance, a complaining spirit. I will often serve a church when asked as a soloist, a speaker to women, or perhaps at Vacation Bible School. I am always happy to serve the Lord where He leads. The one thing that seems to be present at nearly every event (not all, mind you) are a complaining spirit or two. They want to destroy the work of God and bring the spirit of complaining.

No good thing ever comes out of complaining. It serves self and nothing else, and Satan loves it. Picture that old devil sitting beside you smiling and whispering, "Go on! This is great." Another place is ungratefulness. Having a spirit of ungratefulness is like wearing a sign that says, "I deserve this. I have arrived." Say "thank you." Be thankful. Then there are other places such as lack of zeal or commitment or making excuses for one's bad behavior. All these places open the door to a broken relationship with God.

The fact is that Satan tries to tempt us to sin against God our Father. When we listen to Satan's lies and go our own path, this can paint a distorted view of our God, views like "God could never forgive me because I am too bad or too far gone." Or there's the perspective that "God does not love me because of the sin in my life or because of what I have done." Satan also wants us to become prideful and feel entitled, showing little or no respect for others. Isn't it interesting that we will listen to the lies of Satan and ignore the truth of God?

There is something terribly wrong with this kind of thinking. We look at the lives of Nabal, Abigail, and David as reminders of how to behave and not behave. Nabal showed little respect for others and got into a habit of practicing evil (1 Samuel 25:3), and it cost him his life. Nabal had allowed Satan to have some space in his life, and Satan came and took up residence. David was treated badly and reacted with anger. He came close to making a huge mistake but listened to the voice of wisdom God used in Abigail. Satan could have used this opportunity to tarnish David's reputation and hurt innocent people; however, David would not give Satan a place to hang out, and he had to flee.

Abigail realized trouble was headed her way. She could have let the chips fall where there may. She could have held up in the house till the danger was gone, but there were no guarantees. Abigail could have run away, leaving everyone behind. Yet Abigail put on her armor of bravery and did not allow fear or circumstances to cloud her judgment. She was battle strong, and Satan had to flee.

Three people. Three choices. We can all stand in any one of these places. The question is: where will you stand, and with who? We are in a battle, and it is dangerous ground when the Christian forgets this. Christian brothers and sisters need each other. We need the Word of God in our hearts to battle the enemy. One of our greatest tools against Satan is the Word of God. God's Word is complete and true from beginning to end. I have been a student of God's Word for many years and go to His Word for everything. God's Word never leads us astray; nor does His Word disappoint. The problem for us is that so many times we do not spend time reading and exercising God's Word in our lives. Being a child of the King means daily going into His Word and asking Him for His guidance. We also need the power of God by His Holy Spirit working in us and through us to defeat the enemy. These tools give us victory over the evil one.

This study of 1 Samuel 25 has a storehouse of wisdom just ready to be used; unless you apply God's Word to your heart and life, it will be fruitless. And fruitlessness is not the goal; fruitfulness is. This small chapter is to help you remember two things. First, the enemy wants a room in your heart. Lock the door to him and do not give him room. Second, keep an open door to Christ. Explore God's Word. Allow God by His Holy Spirit to show you all He has for you through the study of His Word. You will grow and grow until one day you look back and say, "What a difference the study of God's Word has made in my life."

Psalm 119:11, 105

"Your word I have hidden in my heart, That I might not sin against You ... Your word is a lamp to my feet And a light to my path."

Toni S. Troxell

Conclusion

My hope for this book is that you are thinking by the end. Perhaps you realize you are not alone or you have stuff in your heart God needs to help you with. Maybe you thought no one could see your heart and now realize God can. Perhaps there is a spirit of Nabal you would rather not have. Maybe you see the need to write the résumé God intends for you or perhaps search for the opportunities God has for you.

Are you in? Have you moved ahead of God, only to find out He had a better plan but anger or impatience has gotten in the way? Do you let a spirit of entitlement, self-service, complaining, or bitterness, just to name a few, lead you into wrong decisions? Are you pondering and focused on the task God has for you? When you listen, do you hear? Are you really studying God's Word? Are you believing the lies of Satan rather than the truth of God? If you got here and are thinking more about the Savior and what He has for you, how great is that!

However, don't stop there. Stay in the Word more and more every day. Let your prayer life bloom into brilliant colors of peace, love, joy, and bravery so others can see what Christ is doing in and through you. Let your heart become visible to a lost world who needs a Savior. I am excited for you as God uses you where you are.

To God Be All the Glory!

Study Guide

Chapter 1: Building a Résumé

It's time to write your résumé. Take a few moments to select a life verse. A life verse shares the heart of your walk with the Lord. (Mine is Psalm 90:17.) Your life verse will be the foundation for your résumé. Remember your résumé will not be finished. It is a tool to help you find out how God is using you and perhaps open your heart to His leading. Follow these steps:

1. Write a cover letter (a letter that explains who you are, not a letter to put yourself down or build yourself up). This letter explains the things you like, do, and so forth. Write how God is revealing Himself to you.

2. Write your experiences with the Lord. (If you are a new Christian, write how He saved you. If you have

never found the Lord as your Savior, now is a great time to stop and let Jesus be the Savior of your life.)

3. Now write down your goals. No matter how crazy or how far out there you may think they are, jot them down anyway. God can do anything. Let no one tell you God cannot. He can. And your goal may be just how He plans to do it. This is where your life verse is very important.

4. Now describe your plan. How is God using all these things to lead you? It matters not your age or place in life. God can do anything. Believe the truth in His Word, not the lies of Satan in your ear.

5. Now execute. Pray and ask God to lead you in fulfilling His plan in your life. Find those mature Christians who can help you, stay in His Word, and pray and pray again.

Chapter 2: When Opportunity Comes

You have heard "opportunities don't come along like this very often." In some cases, this may be true. God has appointed God moments for each of us, that is, moments designed that help us minister to others. Abigail saw an opportunity to undo a wrong done by Nabal. She was not about to let the opportunity escape. Many depended on the next step she would take.

This may be the same for us. Here, if you do not have one already, you will start a journal. This is an opportunity journal. For the next week, you will look for opportunities to serve someone else, an opportunity to show a kindness. Yes, you may have to go looking for those God moments, but go looking nonetheless. Pray and ask God to open doors. He will. And then record those open doors. Follow these steps:

1. Find a notebook and write on the front "Opportunity Journal."
2. Every day for the next week, look for those opportunities to show a kindness, serve others, and so on.
3. Record the beginning (how the event came to be) and the outcome (the reaction of the person or people).
4. Write a summary at the end of the week how God used you in these opportunities.
5. Describe what you would do differently and how you will continue to practice what you have learned.
6. One thing to keep in mind—and this may be uncomfortable for some—but do not give up or give in. You may miss being a blessing or receiving a blessing. Be creative. What joy are you about to experience?

Chapter 3: I Got This!

David was ready to take things into his own hands. The thought did not occur to him in his anger that he was about to make a huge mistake. For a few moments, put on David's shoes and answer these questions and follow these steps:

1. How would you have dealt with Nabal and his wickedness? Honest now!
2. Was David correct in his anger?
3. What was fueling David's anger?
4. If Abigail had not interceded, what would David have done?
5. Have you ever been in David's shoes in your life, and how did you handle the situation?
6. Do you have an Abigail in your life? Have you ever been an Abigail to someone else?
7. Have your actions, like that of Nabal, ever put you at odds with another person? Was it resolved peacefully? What does the scripture say about dealing with problems in others? (Be ready to back it up with scripture.)
8. How can you apply these truths to your own life?

Chapter 4: Prerogative

There are always two sides to every story. Yet here we have three sides. Think for a moment about the three people of 1 Samuel 25: Nabal, Abigail, and David. How would each one defends his or her story? Look at each point of view, and bring the setting into today's society. How can you see each one played out in our world today? With each group believing they are correct; how does one determine the right solution? Seeing the outcome in 1 Samuel 25:2–42, what steps could be used today in similar situations? Follow these steps:

1. Examine each of the three people: Nabal, Abigail, and David. What was their goal in their actions?
2. Where in our culture today have you seen these three attitudes? Which attitudes or actions seem to be more prominent in our world today?
3. Can you identify yourself in any or all of these three people: Nabal, Abigail, and David?
4. What was the outcome of your actions as Nabal, David, or Abigail?
5. Can you see any change in your thinking as a result of what you have read in 1Samuel 25:2–42?

Chapter 5: A Focused Heart

Do you find it hard to focus on God's Word? What do you find to be your favorite story in the Bible? If you are up to the challenge, try this for the next four weeks. Find a different Bible lesson every week that you can relate to your life. Follow this outline:

1. Find your story (e.g., Jonah and the whale).
2. In your journal every day, write a truth you have found by reading this truth (i.e., reading that same story every day for a week and writing in your journal every day).
3. Pray and ask God how you can apply this to your life. (Do not pick an evil person and practice their behavior.)
4. Pick a new story for week two, three, and four. Do the same as before.
5. In week five, share with a mature mentor what God has shown you and share what you have learned and how you plan to apply this new behavior to your walk with Christ.

Chapter 6: The Heart Unseen

The word invisible means something you cannot see. We cannot see into the heart of others, but God can. This exercise is a walk with you and the Lord. We all have stuff in our heart that only God can see. Take some time in prayer. You can write it out if you wish or simply talk with the Lord. The idea here is to clean out the spaces that are cluttered. In these quiet moments, talk to the Lord about those things that may be hindering you and your walk with the Lord, for example, hurt feelings, bitterness, anger (with others or God), selfishness, pride, entitlement, revenge, being bullied or being a bully, the past, relationships, trust or love issues, and salvation.

The last is the most important! (After you have opened your heart to the Lord, ask Him what He would have you do and obey His leading. If you are unsure, seek out a mature Christian to help.)

Chapter 7: Listen ... Listen ... Listen

How do you develop the art of listening? That's a good question, and we are about to practice our skills. In this section, we will practice what we learn.

1. In the study guide of chapter five, we wrote out a story in our journals every day for four weeks. Now you will have someone read that story to you and what you have wrote in your journal. You will listen as they read and focus on the story you choose.

2. As you listen, listen to hear something new you did not get before.

3. When the person finishes, discuss how easy or hard this exercise was and how you will apply it in the future when listening to others.

4. Reverse roles now. You read; they listen. How different were your styles? Do you need to improve your listening and hearing skills? If so, how?

Chapter 8: The Sovereignty of God

Define the sovereignty of God. Now answer these questions honestly:

1. Do you believe God and His Word?

2. If so, do you live for Him? Why or why not? What prevents you from believing?

3. How does God feel about our unbelief?

4. What does the sovereignty of God have to do with this book and the outcome of this study? Can accepting this fact change your world? How? What are you going to do now?

The Plan of Salvation through Jesus Christ Our Lord

For God so loved the world that He gave His only begotten Son, that whoever believes in Him should not perish but have everlasting life.

—John 3:16

God's Plan for Salvation

God loves us and has a plan for our lives, and He wants us to be with Him in heaven. However, we are all sinners. "For all have sinned and come short of the glory of God" (Romans 3:23). Sin is anything that is not pleasing to God. One sin keeps us from heaven; therefore, none can go to heaven. Sin breaks our fellowship with God. And the wages for those sins must be paid. "For the wages of sin is death, but the gift of God is eternal life through Jesus Christ our Lord" (Romans 6:23).

But There Is Good … No, Great News

God had a plan. He would send His only perfect Son for the salvation of the world. "For God so loved the world that He gave His only Son, that whosoever believes in Him should not perish but have everlasting life" (John 3:16). Through faith, by believing that Jesus being born of a virgin (Matthew 1:26–38) died, was buried, rose the third day for our sins, and one day come again (1 Corinthians 15:3–8), we receive eternal life "For by grace you have been saved through faith; and that not of yourselves, it is the gift of God; not as a result of works, so that no one may boast" (Ephesians 2:8–9).

No other way can bring salvation but through God's only Son, Jesus "Jesus said to him, 'I am the way, and the truth, and the life; no one comes to the Father but through Me'" (John 14:6). When we pray and ask Jesus to forgive our sins and to come into our life and save us, He will. "Behold, I stand at the door and knock; if anyone hears My voice and opens the door, I will come in to him and will dine with him, and he with Me" (Revelation 3:20).

Accept Jesus as Your Personal Savior

Salvation is God's gift to you through Jesus Christ, but we must accept it. You can pray to Jesus. The prayer of salvation goes something like this, "Jesus, I know I am a sinner. I have sinned against You. Please forgive me of my sins. I believe You died, were buried, rose the third day for my sins, and will come again. Come into my life and save me and be my Lord and Savior. Thank You, Lord, for saving me."

We accept Jesus by faith, and if you prayed this prayer, to God be the glory. I rejoice over you and your victory. Next thing to do is tell someone who will share and encourage you in your walk with Jesus. And find a Bible-believing, Christ-centered church where you can grow with God's people. Let me know about your decision so I can pray for you and rejoice over you.

Bibliography

Henry, M., L.F. Church, and M. Henry, M. *Matthew Henry's Commentary in One Volume: Genesis to Revelation.* Grand Rapids: Zondervan Pub. House, 1999.

"Prerogative." https://dictionary.cambridge.org/us/dictionary/english/prerogative.

The Holy Bible: New King James Version. Nashville, Thomas Nelson, 1982.

Wedgeworth, C., and E. Hulse. "Danny Gokey - Haven't Seen It Yet Lyrics." https://lyricsfa.com/2019/01/12/danny-gokey-havent-seen-it-yet-lyrics.

"What is Celiac Disease?" https://celiac.org/celiac-disease/understanding- celiac-disease-2/what-is-celiac-disease.

Printed in the United States
By Bookmasters